How To Start A Small Food Truck Business
A Food Truck Business Plan, Where To Buy A Lunch Truck & Free Cash Crowdfunding

by Weber Johnson

ABOUT THE AUTHOR

The author of over 100 business start-up guides, real estate investing programs and Christian literature. He started his company as a small software company back in 1992.

He served in the US Army and worked over a decade for the US Postal Service. An active real estate investor, he has also served as a minister for the Churches of Christ in Virginia and Michigan.

He has degree's in Business Administration and Applied Science & Computer Programming.

His books and video training programs have helped thousands of people all over the world start there own successful business.

Copyright © 2019 MahoneyProducts
All rights reserved.

DEDICATION

This book is dedicated to my son's
Christian and Matthew.
A blessing from God and the joy of my life.

Table of Contents

Chapter 1 Business Overview

Chapter 2 A Step by Step Plan

Chapter 3 Business Plan

Chapter 4 Free Money to Get Started

Chapter 5 Colossal Cash from Crowdfunding

Chapter 6 Business Insurance

Chapter 7 Business Legal Structure

Chapter 8 Food Truck Business Rolodex

Chapter 9 Zero Cost Marketing

Chapter 10 Business Terms

ACKNOWLEDGMENTS

I WOULD LIKE TO ACKNOWLEDGE ALL THE HARD WORK OF THE MEN AND WOMEN OF THE UNITED STATES MILITARY, WHO RISK THEIR LIVES ON A DAILY BASIS, TO MAKE THE WORLD A SAFER PLACE.

Chapter 1

Food Truck Business Overview

Food Truck Business Overview

A food truck is a large vehicle equipped to cook and sell food. Some, including ice cream trucks, sell frozen or prepackaged food; others have on-board kitchens and prepare food from scratch. Sandwiches, hamburgers, french fries, and other regional fast food fare is common. In recent years, associated with the pop-up restaurant phenomenon, food trucks offering gourmet cuisine and a variety of specialties and ethnic menus, have become particularly popular. Food trucks, along with portable food kiosks and food carts, are on the front line of the street food industry that serves an estimated 2.5 billion people every day.

Food trucks service events (carnivals, construction sites, sporting events etc.) and places of regular work or study – college campuses, office complexes, industrial parks, auto repair shops, movie sets, farmers' markets, military bases, etc. – where regular meals or snacks are in high demand by potential customers.

Food truck dining has caught on in several U.S. and Canadian cities including Toronto, Montreal, Hamilton, Vancouver, Washington, D.C., New York, Austin, Houston, Los Angeles, San Francisco, Seattle, St. Louis, Calgary, Portland and Tampa.

Food Truck Business Overview

History

In the US, the Texas chuckwagon is a precursor to the American food truck. In the later 1800s, herding cattle from the Southwest to markets in the North and East kept cowhands on the trail for months at a time. In 1866, the "father of the Texas Panhandle," Charles Goodnight, a Texas cattle rancher, fitted a sturdy old United States Army wagon with interior shelving and drawers, and stocked it with kitchenware, food and medical supplies. Food consisted of dried beans, coffee, cornmeal, greasy cloth-wrapped bacon, salt pork, beef, usually dried or salted or smoked, and other easy to preserve food stuffs.

The wagon was also stocked with a water barrel and a sling to kindle wood to heat and cook food.

Another early relative of the modern food truck is the lunch wagon, as conceived by food vendor Walter Scott in 1872. Scott cut windows in a small covered wagon, parked it in front of a newspaper office in Providence Rhode Island, and sold sandwiches, pies and coffee to pressmen and journalists.

Food Truck Business Overview

By the 1880s, former lunch-counter boy, Thomas H. Buckley, was manufacturing lunch wagons in Worcester, Massachusetts. He introduced various models, like the Owl and the White House Cafe, with features that included sinks, refrigerators and cooking stoves, also colored windows and other ornamentation.

Later versions of the food truck were mobile canteens, which were created in the late 1950s. These mobile canteens were authorized by the U.S. Army and operated on stateside army bases.

Mobile food trucks, or "roach coaches," have been around for years, serving construction sites, factories, and other blue-collar locations. In big cities of the U.S. the food truck traditionally provided a means for the on-the-go person to grab a quick bite at a low cost. Food trucks are not only sought out for their affordability but as well for their nostalgia; and their popularity continues to rise.

    In recent years, the food truck resurgence was fueled by a combination of post-recessionary factors. Due to an apparent combination of economic and technological factors combined with street food being "hip" or "chic", there has been an increase in the number of food trucks in the United States.

Food Truck Business Overview

The construction business was drying up, leading to a surplus of food trucks, and chefs from high-end restaurants were being laid off. For experienced cooks suddenly without work, the food truck seemed a clear choice.

Once more commonplace in American coastal big cities like New York and LA, gourmet food trucks are now to be found as well in the suburbs, and in small towns across the country. Food trucks are also being hired for special events, such as weddings, school dances, birthday parties, retirement parties, and such public gatherings as art festivals and movie nights.

The gourmet food truck

A modern-day food truck isn't just an ordinary taco truck one might find at a construction site. In 2009, New York magazine noted that the food truck had "largely transcended its roach-coach classification and is now a respectable venue for aspiring chefs to launch careers." These gourmet trucks' menus run the gamut of ethnic and fusion cuisine. Often focusing on limited but creative dishes at reasonable prices, they offer customers a chance to experience food they otherwise may not. Finding a niche seems to be a path to success for most trucks.

Food Truck Business Overview

While one truck may specialize in outlandish burgers, another may serve only lobster rolls. Food trucks are now even Zagat rated.

Tracking food trucks has become much less difficult. With the help of social media like Facebook and Twitter, a person can find where their favorite gourmet truck will be at any moment and get up-to-the-minute updates on specials, new menu items and location changes. In fact, it could be argued that these social media outlets were the biggest contributing factor to the success of the gourmet food truck. In addition to social media, there are a number of food truck tracking programs for smartphones. Some cover specific geographical regions, and others work everywhere.

Food truck rallies and food truck parks are also growing in popularity in the US. At rallies, people can find their favorite trucks all in one place and as well provide a means for a variety of diverse cultures to come together and find a common ground over a love for food.

Food Truck Business Overview

On August 31, 2013, Tampa hosted the world's largest food truck rally, with 99 trucks attending. And food truck parks, offering permanent locations, are found in urban and suburban areas across the US.

The popularity of food trucks lead to the creation of associations that protect and support their business rights, such as the Philadelphia Mobile Food Association.

Business and Economics

Food trucks are subject to the same range of concerns as other foodservice businesses. They generally require a fixed address to accept delivery of supplies. A commercial kitchen may be needed for food prep. There are a variety of permits to obtain, and a health code to observe. Labor and fuel costs are a significant part of the overhead.

Legal definitions and requirements for food trucks vary widely by country and locality. For example, in Toronto, Canada, some of the requirements include business and liability insurance, a Commercial Vehicle Operator's Registration for the truck, permits for each municipality being operated in (downtown, various suburbs), a food handler certificate, appropriate driver's licenses for drivers, assistant's licenses for assistants, and a health inspection.

Food Truck Business Overview

As the rising number and popularity of food trucks push them into the food mainstream, region by region, problems with local legislators and police reacting to new situations, and brick-and-mortar restaurants fearing competition, have to be worked through, in some cases creating significant business uncertainty. Chicago long held the distinction of being the only city in the United States that did not allow food trucks to cook on board, which required trucks to prepare food in a commercial condition, then wrap and label the food and load it into a food warmer. In 2012, under pressure from food truck owners and supporters, including the University of Chicago Law School, regulations were changed to allow on-board cooking, however, controversially, food trucks are required to park 200 feet away from any restaurant, which virtually eliminates busy downtown locations.

In the US, specialized food truck outfitters offer comprehensive start-up services that can include concept development, training, and business support, in addition to outfitted trucks.

Expansion from a single truck to fleets and retail outlets has proven possible. Los Angeles-based gourmet ice cream maker Coolhaus grew from a single truck in 2009 to 11 trucks and carts, two storefronts, and over 2,500 retail partner stores by September 2014.

Food Truck Business Overview

Asia

In Asia, the cuisine offered by food trucks requires simple skills, basic facilities and a relatively small amount of capital. They are plentiful, with large potential for income and often a very large sector for employment. Individuals facing difficulty finding work in formal sectors, will often venture into this industry, as it allows entire families to involve themselves in the preparing and cooking of foods sold to the public. The appeal involved in sustaining a food truck lie not only in the low capital requirement, but also in the flexibility of hours, with minimal constraints to locale. Street foods predominantly reflect local culture and flavor.

Food trucks appeal to consumers in that they are often an inexpensive means of attaining quick meals. Location and word of mouth promotion has been credited for their widening success.

Food Truck Business Overview

Belgium

Potato chip ("french" fries) trucks have been a staple of the Belgian country-side for ages. The lobbying "Belgian Food Truck Association" to contribute to legalize food trucks in the streets. The city of Brussels was the first European city to propose locations for trucks football. It esy in Belgium that is the largest Festival of Food Trucks Europe (Brussels Food Truck festival) every year in May.

Canada

Bud the Spud in Halifax, Nova Scotia.

In Canada, food trucks, also commonly known as cantines (French for cafeteria) in Quebec, are present across the country, serving a wide variety of cuisines, including anything from grilled cheese sandwiches to Mexican.

In 2013, Vancouver-based food truck, Vij's Railway Express, serving fresh Indian cuisine, won the People's Choice award for Canada's best new restaurant of the year, in national airline Air Canada's enRoute Magazine poll, facing off in the finals against 34 conventional restaurants.

Food Truck Business Overview

France

Although food trucks are common at outdoor markets, American-style trucks selling restaurant-quality food first appeared in Paris in 2012. Their owners needed to obtain permission from four separate government agencies, including the Prefecture of Police, but the trucks' offerings—including tacos and hamburgers—have reportedly been very popular.

Mexico

Although street food in Mexico is illegal and unregulated, food trucks are becoming increasingly popular as of 2013 and owners have created an association to pursue the professionalization and expansion of this commercial sector. In addition to the food trucks catering on the streets, there are regular bazaars organized to introduce their products to the consumers.

In response to this popularity the Local Authorities have issued a series of special regulations to incorporate them to legal schemes that would help to order this commerce form. as new food truck business model emerged, some local body-builders begin to make food trucks from new vehicles from major car-makers.

Food Truck Business Overview

United Kingdom

With the advent of motorised transport during World War II, food trucks came into common use. Mobile canteens were used in almost all theatres of war to boost morale and provide food as a result of the successful tea lady experiment.

Food trucks today are known as snack vans and can be found on nearly all major trunk roads at the side of the road or in areas that have a large pedestrian population, such as at village fetes or town centers. These vans can specialise in myriad different food types, such as donuts, hamburgers, chili and chips, as well as ethnic food. Some people prefer to stop at snack vans when travelling, due to the low price, rather than stop at a motorway service station where prices can be extremely high.

Food Truck Business Overview

In popular culture

In the United States, the food truck phenomenon can be seen regularly on national food television Both The Great Food Truck Race (a reality series on the Food Network) and Eat St. (broadcast on the sister station, Cooking Channel), feature food trucks and mobile food carts from all over the US. The Food Network show Kid in a Candy Store also visited food trucks, looking behind the scenes of gourmet dessert truck Coolhaus to show Balsamic Fig & Mascarpone ice cream in the making.

On Canada's Food Network, Food Truck Face Off, four teams battle for the grand prize, use of a customized food truck for one year.

In the 2014 American comedy-drama, **Chef,** a high-end chef has a kitchen meltdown and rediscovers his passion for cooking while driving and operating a simple food truck across America. (EXCELLENT MOVIE!!!)

Food Truck Business Overview

BUYING A FOOD-TRUCK

(USE THE WEB RESOURCE FOR WHOLESALE/DISCOUNT TRUCK DEALS!)

Once you are able to buy a food truck, have a mechanic you can trust, that will be ready to fix your truck quickly should it break down. You might even want to have more than one truck so you don't lose business while one is getting repaired.

Here is a guideline that you can take if you want to buy a food truck:

Be willing to look into a used truck before purchasing a new truck. Learn what the food vending essentials are for your area, from other food trucks and those who sold or sell to them.

If you buy a used truck have a mechanic look it over for you. It is too big a an investment not to.

 Test drive your truck and make sure it is easy to maneuver.

Do your research. Know what a good price is for your truck and be willing to travel out of your area if the deal is good enough.

Food Truck Business Overview

10 Steps for FOOD TRUCK Success

1. Lay a good business foundation by following the step by step instructions in the other section of this book.

2. Purchase a good truck and all of your cooking equipment.

3. Try to use the freshes food possible every day.

4. Don't reinvent the wheel at first. Study the most successful food trucks and emulate them.

5. Watch the movie Chef... If that does not motivatate/excite you, this is not for you.

6. A great Chef once said "if my cooking is only as good as mama's why should they leave the home and come to my restaurant." Make your food taste better than home cooking!

7. Begin with Zero Cost Marketing, but also keep flyers and cards to pass out and promote your business.

Food Truck Business Overview

8. Learn Social Media. Promote on Facebook, YouTube and Pinterest.

9. Write and submit a press release. If you don't know how, go to www.fiverr.com and get one written for only $5.00 the google "free press release submission" to get it out there for free.

10. Contact your local news media(with a press kit) when you are ready to be interviewed.

Food Truck Business Overview

Top 9 Food Truck Businesses

According to CNBC/Susan Caminiti these are the top 10 Food Truck businesses in the United States. Don't try to reinvent the wheel. Look at these successful businesses and model your business after what you think are their best features.

1. Oink & Moo BBQ, Florham Park, New Jersey

http://oinkandmoobbq.com/

2. Cinnamon Snail, New York City

http://cinnamonsnail.com/

3. Ms. Cheezious, Miami

4. Kogi BBQ, Los Angeles

http://kogibbq.com/

5. The Cow and Curd, Philadelphia

http://thecowandthecurd.com/

6. Luke's Lobster, New York City

https://www.lukeslobster.com/

Food Truck Business Overview

Top 9 Food Truck Businesses

7. Mac Mart Truck, Philadelphia

https://macmartcart.com/

8. Fukuburger Truck, Las Vegas

http://www.fukuburger.com/

9. Grilled Cheeserie, Nashville, Tennessee

https://grilledcheeserie.com/

A few things these businesses have in common is a well designed web site. Look at the similarity of each web site's design. Study the menu's on each site. What are the demographic's of each location?

Get as many success secrets from these Food Truck Business's that are thriving. Mix in with your own passion, and you will be on your way to stacking the odds in your favor for having a successful business!

Chapter 2

How To Get Started Step by Step

How to Get Started Step by Step

Starting a business involves planning, making key financial decisions and completing a series of legal activities. These 12 easy steps can help you plan, prepare and manage your business.

Step 1: Write a Business Plan

Use these tools and resources to create a business plan. This written guide will help you map out how you will start and run your business successfully.

Step 2: Get Business Assistance and Training

Take advantage of free training and counseling services, from preparing a business plan and securing financing, to expanding or relocating a business from the Small Business Administration.

Step 3: Choose a Business Location

Get advice on how to select a customer-friendly location and comply with zoning laws.

Step 4: Finance Your Business

Find government backed loans, venture capital and research grants to help you get started.

How to Get Started Step by Step

Step 5: Determine the Legal Structure of Your Business Decide which form of ownership is best for you: sole proprietorship, partnership, Limited Liability Company (LLC), corporation, S corporation, nonprofit or cooperative.

Step 6: Register a Business Name ("Doing Business As") Register your business name with your state government.

Step 7: Get a Tax Identification Number

Learn which tax identification number you'll need to obtain from the IRS and your state revenue agency.

Step 8: Register for State and Local Taxes

Register with your state to obtain a tax identification number, workers' compensation, unemployment and disability insurance.

Step 9: Obtain Business Licenses and Permits

Get a list of federal, state and local licenses and permits required for your business.

Step 10: Understand Employer Responsibilities

Learn the legal steps you need to take to hire employees.

How to Get Started Step by Step

Step 11: Get Equipment and Supplies

Get everything together that you'll need in order to actually operate. This includes items such as a truck, chemicals, equipment, and the various business forms such as service contracts. Once you have these things together, you can start the marketing process in order to get new customers. The Rolodex in the book has great places to find these items at great prices!

Step 12: Your Marketing Plan

Coming up with your overall marketing plan, and implementing that plan. When you're just starting, it is usually best to choose one or two major marketing strategies, and work on those until you're getting a steady stream of customers. Once you've gotten good at once specific marketing avenue, then it's a good idea to move on to another one, and repeat the process. You can begin with "Zero cost marketing" and scale up once you are bringing in constant sales.

Chapter 3
How to Write a Business Plan

How to Write a Business Plan

Millions of people want to know what is the secret to making money. Most have come to the conclusion that it is to start a business. So how to start a business? The first thing you do to start is business is to create a business plan.

A business plan is a formal statement of a set of business goals, the reasons they are believed attainable, and the plan for reaching those goals. It may also contain background information about the organization or team attempting to reach those goals.

A professional business plan consists of ten parts.

1. Executive Summary

The executive summary is often considered the most important section of a business plan. This section briefly tells your reader where your company is, where you want to take it, and why your business idea will be successful. If you are seeking financing, the executive summary is also your first opportunity to grab a potential investor's interest.

How to Write a Business Plan

2. Company Description

This section of your plan provides a high-level review of the different elements of your business. This is akin to an extended elevator pitch and can help readers and potential investors quickly understand the goal of your business and its unique proposition.

3. Market Analysis

The market analysis section of your plan should illustrate your industry and market knowledge as well as any of your research findings and conclusions. This section is usually presented after the company description.

4. Organization and Management

Organization and Management follows the Market Analysis. This section should include: your company's organizational structure, details about the ownership of your company, profiles of your management team, and the qualifications of your board of directors.

How to Write a Business Plan

5. Service or Product Line

Once you've completed the Organizational and Management section of your plan, the next part of your plan is where you describe your service or product, emphasizing the benefits to potential and current customers. Focus on why your particular product will fill a need for your target customers.

6. Marketing and Sales

Once you've completed the Service or Product Line section of your plan, the next part of your plan should focus on your marketing and sales management strategy for your business.

7. Funding Request

If you are seeking funding for your business venture, use this section to outline your requirements.

How to Write a Business Plan

8. Financial Projections

You should develop the Financial Projections section after you've analyzed the market and set clear objectives. That's when you can allocate resources efficiently. The following is a list of the critical financial statements to include in your business plan packet.

9. Marketing and Sales

Once you've completed the Service or Product Line section of your plan, the next part of your business plan should focus on your marketing and sales management strategy for your business.

How to Write a Business Plan

10. Appendix

The Appendix should be provided to readers on an as-needed basis. In other words, it should not be included with the main body of your business plan. Your plan is your communication tool; as such, it will be seen by a lot of people. Some of the information in the business section you will not want everyone to see, but specific individuals (such as creditors) may want access to this information to make lending decisions. Therefore, it is important to have the appendix within easy reach.

How to make your business plan stand out.

One of the first steps to business planning is determining your target market and why they would want to buy from you.

For example, is the market you serve the best one for your product or service? Are the benefits of dealing with your business clear and are they aligned with customer needs? If you're unsure about the answers to any of these questions, take a step back and revisit the foundation of your business plan.

These tips can help you clarify what your business has to offer, identify the right target market for it and build a niche for yourself.

Chapter 4

Goldmine of Government Grants

How to write a Winning Grant Proposal

Goldmine of Government Grants

Government grants. Many people either don't believe government grants exist or they don't think they would ever be able to get government grant money.

First lets make one thing clear. Government grant money is **YOUR MONEY**. Government money comes from taxes paid by residents of this country. Depending on what state you live in, you are paying taxes on almost everything....Property tax for your house. Property tax on your car. Taxes on the things you purchase in the mall, or at the gas station. Taxes on your gasoline, the food you buy etc.

So get yourself in the frame of mind that you are not a charity case or too proud to ask for help, because billionaire companies like GM, Big Banks and most of Corporate America is not hesitating to get their share of **YOUR MONEY**!

There are over two thousand three hundred (2,300) Federal Government Assistance Programs. Some are loans but many are formula grants and project grants. To see all of the programs available go to:

https://beta.sam.gov/help/assistance-listing

WRITING A GRANT PROPOSAL

The Basic Components of a Proposal

There are eight basic components to creating a solid proposal package:

1. The proposal summary;
2. Introduction of organization;
3. The problem statement (or needs assessment);
4. Project objectives;
5. Project methods or design;
6. Project evaluation;
7. Future funding; and
8. The project budget.

WRITING A GRANT PROPOSAL

The Proposal Summary

The Proposal Summary is an outline of the project goals and objectives. Keep the Proposal Summary short and to the point. No more that 2 or 3 paragraphs. Put it at the beginning of the proposal.

Introduction

The Introduction portion of your grant proposal presents you and your business as a credible applicant and organization.

Highlight the accomplishments of your organization from all sources: newspaper or online articles etc. Include a biography of key members and leaders. State the goals and philosophy of the company.

The Problem Statement

The problem statement makes clear the problem you are going to solve(maybe reduce homelessness). Make sure to use facts. State who and how those affected will benefit from solving the problem. State the exact manner in how you will solve the problem.

WRITING A GRANT PROPOSAL

Project Objectives

The Project Objectives section of your grant proposal focuses on the Goals and Desired outcome.

Make sure to indentify all objectives and how you are going to reach these objectives. The more statistics you can find to support your objectives the better. Make sure to put in realistic objectives. You may be judged on how well you accomplish what you said you intended to do.

Program Methods and Design

The program methods and design section of your grant proposal is a detailed plan of action.

>What resources are going to be used.

>What staff is going to be needed.

>System development.

>Create a Flow Chart of project features.

>Explain what will be achieved.

>Try to produce evidence of what will be achieved.

>Make a diagram of program design.

WRITING A GRANT PROPOSAL

Evaluation

There is product evaluation and process evaluation. The product evaluation deals with the result that relate to the project and how well the project has met it's objectives.

The process evaluation deals with how the project was conducted, how did it line up with the original stated plan and the overall effectiveness of the different aspects of the plan.

Evaluations can start at anytime during the project or at the project's conclusion. It is advised to submit a evaluation design at the start of a project.

 It looks better if you have collected convincing data before and during the program.

If evaluation design is not presented at the beginning that might encourage a critical review of the program design.

Future Funding

The Future Funding part of the grant proposal should have long term project planning past the grant period.

WRITING A GRANT PROPOSAL

Budget

Utilities, rental equipment, staffing, salary, food, transportation, phone bills and insurance are just some of the things to include in the budget.

A well constructed budget accounts for every penny.

For a complete guide for government grants google catalog of federal domestic assistance. You can download a complete PDF version of the catalog.

Other sources of Government Funding

You can get General Small Business loans from the government. Go to the Small Business Administration for more information.

SBA Microloan Program

The Microloan program provides loans of up to $50,000 with the average loan being $13,000.

https://www.sba.gov/

WRITING A GRANT PROPOSAL

Recently billionaire Elon Musk was awarded 4.9 billion dollars in government subsidies. If you are hesitant to pursue government assistance, let that sink in. A billionaire who pays little in taxes was given billions of your tax dollars.

Government grants are real. Like anything else worthwhile, there is effort and qualifications that must be met to obtain them.

Chapter 5

Colossal Cash

from

Crowd Funding

Crowd Funding Crowd Sourcing

In 2015 over $34 billion dollars was raised by crowdfunding. Crowdfunding and Crowdsourcing roots began in 2005 and they help to finance or fund projects by raising money from a large number of people, usually by using the internet.

This type of fundraising or venture capital usually has 3 components. The individual or organization with a project that needs funding, groups of people who donate to the project, and a organization sets up a structure or rules to put the two together.

These websites do charge fees. The standard fee for success is about %5. If your goal is not met there is also a fee.

Below is a list of the top Crowdfunding websites according to myself and Entrepreneur Magazine Contributor Sally Outlaw.

Crowd Funding Crowd Sourcing

https://www.indiegogo.com/

Started as a platform for getting movies made, now helps to raise funds for any cause.

http://rockethub.com/

Started as a platform for the arts, now it helps to raise funds for business, science, social projects and education.

http://peerbackers.com/

Peerbackers focuses on raising funds for business, entrepreneurs and innovators.

https://www.kickstarter.com/

The most popular and well know n of all the crowdfunding websites. Kickstarter focuses on film, music, technology, gaming, design and the creative arts. Kickstarter only accepts projects from the United States, Canada and the United Kingdom.

Crowd Funding Crowd Sourcing

Group Growvc

http://group.growvc.com/

This website is for business and technology innovation.

https://microventures.com/

Get access to angel investors. This website is for business startups.

https://angel.co/

Another website for business startups.

https://circleup.com/

Circle up is for innovative consumer companies.

https://www.patreon.com/

If you start a YouTube Channel (highly recommended) you will hear about this website frequently. This website is for creative content people.

Crowd Funding Crowd Sourcing

https://www.crowdrise.com/

"Raise money for any cause that inspires you." The Landing page slogan speaks for itself. #1 fundraising website for personal causes.

https://www.gofundme.com/

This fundraising website allows for business, charity, education, emergencies, sports, medical, memorials, animals, faith, family, newlyweds etc...

https://www.youcaring.com/

The leader in free fundraising. Over $400 million raised.

https://fundrazr.com/

FundRazr is an award-winning online fundraising platform that has helped thousands of people and organizations raise money
for causes they care about.

CHAPTER 6
Business Insurance

BUSINESS INSURANCE

Consult an attorney for any and all of your business matters.

In the early 1990's an elderly woman purchased a hot cup of coffee from a McDonald's drive-thru window in Albuquerque. She spilled the coffee, and suffered 3rd degree burns. She sued Mcdonald's and won. She won 2.7 million dollars in a punitive damages victory. The verdict was appealed and settlement is estimated at somewhere in the neighborhood of $500,000 dollars. All because she spilled the coffee into her lap, while trying to add sugar and cream.

Two men in Ohio, were carpet layers. They were severely burned when a three and a half gallon container of carpet adhesive ignited, when the hot water heater it was sitting next to, was turned on. They felt the warning lable on the back of the can was insufficient. So they filed a lawsuit against the adhesive manufacturers and were awarded nine million dollars.

A woman in Oklahoma, purchased a brand new Winnebago. While driving it home, she set the cruise control to 70 miles per hour. She then left the drivers seat to make some coffee or a sandwich in the back of the motor home.

BUSINESS INSURANCE

The vehicle crashed and the woman sued Winnebago for not advising her, that cruise control does not drive and steer the vehicle. She won 1.7 million dollars and the company had to rewrite their instruction manual.

Unfortunately all three outrageous lawsuits are real. If you are going to run a business, any business, you should consider protecting yourself with Professional Liability Insurance, also known as Errors and Omissions (E & 0) insurance.

This type of insurance can help to protect you from having to pay the full cost of defending yourself against a negligence lawsuit claim.

Error and Omissions can protect you against claims that are not usually covered in regular liability insurance. Those policies usually cover bodily harm, or damage to property. Error and Omissions can protect you agaist negligence, and other mental anguish like inaccurate advice, or misrepresentation. Criminal prosecution is not covered.

Errors and Ommision insurance is recommended for notaries public, real estate brokers or investors and professionals like: software engineers, lawyers, home inspectors web site delvelopers and landscape architects to name a few professions.

BUSINESS INSURANCE

The Most Common Errors and Omission Claims:

%25 Breach of Fiduciary Duty

%15 Breach of Contract

%14 Negligence

%13 Failure to Supervise

%11 Unsuitability

%10 Other

BUSINESS INSURANCE

Things you should know about or require before purchasing a Errors and Omission policy is...

* What is the limit of liability

* What is the Deductible

* Does it include FDD First Dollar Defense - which obligates the insurance company to fight a case without a deductible first.

* Do I have Tail-end coverage or Extended Reporting Coverage (insurance that lasts into retirement)

* Extended coverage for Employees

* Cyber Liability Coverage

* Department of Labor Fiduciary Coverage

* Insolvency Coverage

If you get Errors and Omission insurance, renew it the day it expires. You must be careful to avoid gaps in your coverage, or it could result in not getting your policy renewed.

BUSINESS INSURANCE

A few E & O Insurance Providers:

Insureon

Insureon states that their median Errors and Omissions Insurance policy cost about $750 a year or about $65 a month. The price of course will vary according to your business, the policy you choose and other risk factors.

https://www.insureon.com/home

EOforless

EOforless.com helps insurance, investment, and real estate professionals buy E & O insurance at an affordable cost in five minutes or less.

https://www.eoforless.com/

BUSINESS INSURANCE

CalSurance Associates

As a leading insurance broker, CalSurance Associates, a division of Brown & Brown Program Insurance Services, Inc. has over fifty years of experience delivering comprehensive insurance products, exceptional service, and proven results to over 150,000 insured. They provide professionals nationwide and across multiple industries, including some of the largest financial firms and insurance companies in the United States.

http://www.calsurance.com/csweb/index.aspx

Better Safe Than Sorry

Insurance is one of the hidden costs of doing business. These are just a few companies and a brief overview on the topic of business insurance. Make sure to talk to an attorney or quailified insurance agent before making any decision on insurance. Protect you and your business. Many states do not require E & O insurances. But when you see the cost of some of the settlements, it's better to be safe than sorry.

Chapter 7

Business Legal Structure

Business Legal Structure

When you are starting a business, one of the first decisions you have to make is the type of business you want to create. A sole proprietorship? A corporation? A limited liability company? This decision is important, because the type of business you create determines the types of applications you’ll need to submit. You should also research liability implications for personal investments you make into your business, as well as the taxes you will need to pay. It’s important to understand each business type and select the one that is best suited for your situation and objectives. Keep in mind that you may need to contact several federal agencies, as well as your state business entity registration office.

Business Legal Structure

Here is a list of the most common ways to structure a business.

An S corporation (sometimes referred to as an S Corp) is a special type of corporation created through an IRS tax election. An eligible domestic corporation can avoid double taxation (once to the corporation and again to the shareholders) by electing to be treated as an S corporation.

A partnership is a single business where two or more people share ownership.

Each partner contributes to all aspects of the business, including money, property, labor or skill. In return, each partner shares in the profits and losses of the business.

A limited liability company is a hybrid type of legal structure that provides the limited liability features of a corporation and the tax efficiencies and operational flexibility of a partnership.

Business Legal Structure

The "owners" of an LLC are referred to as "members." Depending on the state, the members can consist of a single individual (one owner), two or more individuals, corporations or other LLCs.

Corporation (C Corporation)

A corporation (sometimes referred to as a C corporation) is an independent legal entity owned by shareholders. This means that the corporation itself, not the shareholders that own it, is held legally liable for the actions and debts the business incurs.

Corporations are more complex than other business structures because they tend to have costly administrative fees and complex tax and legal requirements. Because of these issues, corporations are generally suggested for established, larger companies with multiple employees.

Business Legal Structure

A cooperative is a business or organization owned by and operated for the benefit of those using its services. Profits and earnings generated by the cooperative are distributed among the members, also known as user-owners.

Typically, an elected board of directors and officers run the cooperative while regular members have voting power to control the direction of the cooperative. Members can become part of the cooperative by purchasing shares, though the amount of shares they hold does not affect the weight of their vote.

Chapter 8

WEB RESOURCE GUIDE
Food Truck Business Rolodex

Food Truck Business Rolodex

FOOD TRUCK/CATERING SUPPLIES

http://www.gourmetstreets.com

http://goo.gl/AjKEw7

http://goo.gl/RcWyX5

http://www.ebay.com/bhp/food-truck

https://www.acemart.com/

http://www.cateringsupplies.com/

http://www.cateringplanet.com/

http://www.catererswarehouse.com/

http://goo.gl/HbT3xk

Food Truck Business Rolodex

FOOD

http://goo.gl/W9lPPb

http://www.dutchvalleyfoods.com/

http://www.primafoodsinc.com/wholesale_food_distributor.asp

TRANSPORTATION

http://www.best-concession-trailer.com/

http://foodtrucks.net/

Food Truck Business Rolodex

Used Trucks Online

http://gsaauctions.gov/gsaauctions/gsaauctions/

http://www.ebay.com/motors

http://www.uhaul.com/TruckSales/

http://www.usedtrucks.ryder.com/vehicle/VehicleSearch.aspx?VehicleTypeId=1&VehicleGroupId=3

http://www.penskeusedtrucks.com/truck-types/light-and-medium-duty/

Parts

http://www.truckchamp.com/

http://www.autopartswarehouse.com/

Food Truck Business Rolodex

Trucking Software

http://goo.gl/1Ye2es

http://goo.gl/4eJPO6

http://goo.gl/AhpU1I

http://www.foglinesoftware.com/

Bikes & Motorcycles

http://gsaauctions.gov/gsaauctions/aucindx/

http://www.bikesdirect.com/products/used-bikes/?gclid=CLCF0vaDm7kCFYtDMgodzW0AXQ

http://www.overstock.com/Sports-Toys/Cycling/450/cat.html

http://www.nashbar.com/bikes/TopCategories_10053_10052_-1

http://www.bti-usa.com/

http://evosales.com/

Food Truck Business Rolodex

COMPUTERS/Office Equipment

http://www.wtsmedia.com/

http://www.laptopplaza.com/

http://www.outletpc.com/

Computer Tool Kits

http://www.dhgate.com/wholesale/computer+repair+tools.html

http://www.aliexpress.com/wholesale/wholesale-repair-computer-tool.html

http://wholesalecomputercables.com/Computer-Repair-Tool-Kit/M/B00006OXGZ.htm

http://www.amazon.com/Wholesale-Computer-Repair-Screwdriver-Insert/dp/B009KV1MM0

http://www.tigerdirect.com/applications/category/category_tlc.asp?CatId=47&name=Computer%20Tools

Food Truck Business Rolodex

Computer Parts

http://www.laptopuniverse.com/

http://www.sabcal.com/

other

http://www.nearbyexpress.com/

http://www.commercialbargains.co

http://www.getpaid2workfromhome.com

http://www.boyerblog.com/success-tools

american merchandise liquidators

http://www.amlinc.com/

the closeout club

http://www.thecloseoutclub.com/

RJ discount sales

http://www.rjsks.com/

Food Truck Business Rolodex

St louis wholesale

http://www.stlouiswholesale.com/

Wholesale Electronics

http://www.weisd.com/

ana wholesale

http://www.anawholesale.com/

office wholesale

http://www.1-computerdesks.com/

1aaa wholesale merchandise

http://www.1aaawholesalemerchandise.com/

big lots wholesale

http://www.biglotswholesale.com/

Food Truck Business Rolodex

More Business Resources

1. http://www.sba.gov/content/starting-green-business

home based businesses

2. http://www.sba.gov/content/home-based-business

3. online businesses

http://www.sba.gov/content/setting-online-business

4. self employed and independent contractors

http://www.sba.gov/content/self-employed-independent-contractors

5. minority owned businesses

http://www.sba.gov/content/minority-owned-businesses

6. veteran owned businesses

http://www.sba.gov/content/veteran-service-disabled-veteran-owned

Food Truck Business Rolodex

7. woman owned businesses

http://www.sba.gov/content/women-owned-businesses

8. people with disabilities

http://www.sba.gov/content/people-with-disabilities

9. young entrepreneurs

http://www.sba.gov/content/young-entrepreneurs

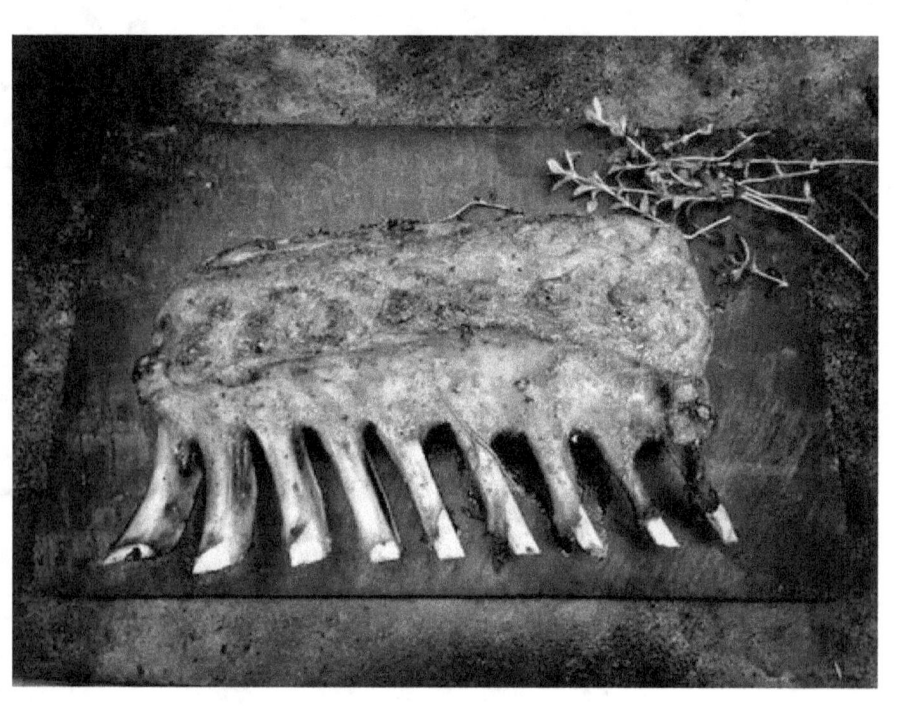

Chapter 9

Zero Cost Business Launch Formula

ZERO COST MARKETING

While there are many ways to market we are only going focus on ZERO COST MARKETING. You are starting up. You can always go for the more expensive ways of marketing after your business is producing income.

FREE WEB HOSTING

Get a free web site. You can get a free web site at weebly.com or wix.com. Or just type "free web hosting" in a google, bing or yahoo search engine.

Free web hosting is something you can use for a varitey or reasons. However many free web hosting sites add an extention to the name of your web address that lets everyone know you are using their services. For this reason you eventually want to scale up once you start making income.

LOW COST PAID WEB HOSTING

Free is nice, but you when you need to expand your business it is best to go with a paid web hosting service. There are several that give you good value for under $10.00 a month.

1. Yahoo small business
2. Intuit.com
3. ipage.com
4. Hostgator.com
5. Godaddy.com

Yahoo small business allows for unlimited web pages and is probably the best overall value, but they require a years payment up front. Intuit allows for monthly payments.

For free ecommerce on your web site, open up a Paypal account and get the HTML code for payment buttons for free. Then put those buttons on your web site.

Step by Step basic zero cost web site traffic instructions

Step 1 zero cost internet marketing

Now that your web site is up and running you should register it with at least the top 3 search engines. 1. Google 2. Bing 3. Yahoo.

Step 2 zero cost internet marketing

Write and submit a **press release**. Google "free press release sites" for press release sites that will allow you to summit press releases for free. If you do not know how to write a press release go to www.fiverr.com and sub-contract the work out for only $5.00 !!!

Step 3 zero cost internet marketing

Write and submit articles to article marketing web sites like **ezinearticles.com.**

Step 4 zero cost internet marketing

Create and submit videos to video sharing sites like dailymotion.com or **youtube.com.** Make sure to include a hyperlink to your website in the description of your videos.

Step 5 zero cost internet marketing

Submit your web site to **dmoz.org**. This is a huge open directory that many smaller search engines go to get web sites for their database.

ZERO COST MARKETING

In an interview with Tom Bilyeu Multi-millionaire Rahel Hollis, the author of "Girl wash your face", said that every thing she that taught her how to build her multi-million dollar empire, she learned from watching free YouTube videos.

You can start a successful business without spending a bunch of money. You just have to gain the proper knowledge and be willing to do "what ever it takes" to succeed!

Chapter 10

Business Terms

Business Terms & Definitions

Accounts – Companies produce a annual set of accounts. If you are listed on the stock exchange you have to give info on profits six months into the financial year.

Actuary – Actuaries work for insurance companies and pension providers and calculate life expectancy, accident rates and likely payouts by using math algorithms.

Business Plan – A business plan is a formal statement of business goals, reasons they are attainable, and plans for reaching them. It may also contain background information about the organization or team attempting to reach those goals.

Balance Sheet – a statement of the assets, liabilities, and capital of a business or other organization at a particular point in time, detailing, the balance of income and expenditure over the preceding period.

Business Terms & Definitions

Bear Market – A stock market in which share prices fall precipitously, typically 15%-20%.

Bull Market – A market when prices roar ahead.

Capital Gains – A capital gain refers to profit that results from a sale of a capital asset, such as stock, bond or real estate, where the sale price exceeds the purchase price. The gain is the difference between a higher selling price and a lower purchase price.

Capital Gains Tax – a tax levied on profit from the sale of property or of an investment.

Chapter 11 Bankruptcy – Chapter 11 is a chapter of Title 11 of the United States Bankruptcy Code, which permits reorganization under the bankruptcy laws of the United States. Chapter 11 bankruptcy is available to every business, whether organized as a corporation, partnership or sole proprietorship, and to individuals, although it is most prominently used by corporate entities.

Business Terms & Definitions

Consumers Prices Index – The Consumer Price Index (CPI) is a measure that examines the weighted average of prices of a basket of consumer goods and services, such as transportation, food and medical care. It is calculated by taking price changes for each item in the predetermined basket of goods and averaging them.

Day Trading - Day Trading is the buying and selling of stocks during the trading day buy punters on their own account. The aim is to make a profit on the day and have no open positions at the close of the trading session.

Dow Jones Industrial Average – The Dow Jones Industrial Average (DJIA) is a price-weighted average of 30 significant stocks traded on the New York Stock Exchange (NYSE) and the NASDAQ. The DJIA was invented by Charles Dow back in 1896.

Diminishing Returns – used to refer to a point at which the level of profits or benefits gained is less than the amount of money or energy invested.

Business Terms & Definitions

Economic Growth – Economic growth is the increase in the inflation adjusted market value of the goods and services produced by an economy over time. It is conventionally measured as the percent rate of increase in real gross domestic product or real GDP.

Equity – the value of the shares issued by a company.

Elasticity – elasticity is a measure of a variable's sensitivity to a change in another variable. In business and economics, elasticity refers the degree to which individuals, consumers or producers change their demand or the amount supplied in response to price or income changes.

Fiscal Year – The US fiscal year runs from October 1 to September 30.

Foreign Exchange (Forex) – Foreign exchange, or forex, markets are where one currency is exchanged for another.

Business Terms & Definitions

FORM 501 – A 501(c) organization is a nonprofit organization in the federal law of the United States according to 26 U.S.C. 501 and is one of 29 types of nonprofit organizations which are exempt from some federal income taxes.

Form 701 – General Information. Registration of a Limited Liability Partnership.

Grant – Grants are non-repayable funds or products disbursed or gifted by one party (grant makers), often a government department, corporation, foundation or trusts to a recipient, often (but not always) a nonprofit entity, educational institution, business or an individual.

Gross Domestic Product – GDP is the sum of all goods and services produced in the economy, including the service sector, manufacturing, construction, energy, agriculture and government.

Business Terms & Definitions

Gross National Product – the total value of goods produced and services provided by a country during one year, equal to the gross domestic product plus the net income from foreign investments.

Hedge Funds – a limited partnership of investors that uses high risk methods, such as investing with borrowed money, in hopes of realizing large capital gains.

Income Statement – An income statement is one of the financial statements of a company and shows the company's revenues and expenses during a particular period.

Income Tax – tax levied by a government directly on income, especially an annual tax on personal income.

Inheritance Tax – a tax imposed on someone who inherits property or money.

Business Terms & Definitions

Inflation – a general increase in prices and fall in the purchasing value of money.

Limited Liability Company (LLC) – A limited liability company (LLC) is a corporate structure whereby the members of the company cannot be held personally liable for the company's debts or liabilities. Limited liability companies are essentially hybrid entities that partnership or sole proprietorship.

Loan to Value – The loan-to-value (LTV) ratio is a financial term used by lenders to express the ratio of a loan to the value of an asset purchased. The term is commonly used by banks and building societies to represent the ration of the first mortgage line as a percentage of the total appraised value of real property.

Microloan – a small sum of money lent at low interest to a new business.

Business Terms & Definitions

Mutual Fund – an investment program funded by shareholders that trades in diversified holdings and is professionally managed.

NASDAQ – The National Association of Securities Dealers Automated Quotations (NASDAQ) was set up in 1971 as an international screen-based trading system without a central dealing floor. In 1998 it merged with the American Stock exchange (Amex).

Occupational Pension Scheme – Occupational pension schemes may be contributory or non-contributory, funded or unfunded, defined benefit or defined contribution. In contributory schemes, both you and your employer pay contributions towards the scheme. In non-contributory schemes, you do not contribute buy your employer does.

Partnership – A legal form of business operation between tow or more individuals who share management and profits. The federal government recognizes several types of partnerships. The two most common are general and limited partnerships. A limited partnership has both general and limited partners.

Business Terms & Definitions

Rate of Return – A rate of return is the gain or loss on an investment over a specified time period, expressed as a percentage of the investment's cost. Gains on investments are defined as income received plus any capital gains realized on the sale of the investment.

Real Estate Investment Trusts – A real estate investment trust (REIT) is a company that owns, and in most cases operates, income-producing real estate. REITs own many types of commercial real estate, ranging from office and apartment buildings to warehouses, shopping centers and hotels.

SBA - The Small Business Administration (SBA0 is a U.S. Government agency, formulated in 1953, that operates autonomously. This agency was established to bolster and promote the economy in general by providing assistance to small businesses.

Business Terms & Definitions

SCORE (SBA) – SCORE is a nonprofit organization that provides free business mentoring services to prospective and established small business owners in the United States. More than 10,000 volunteers provide these services, with all volunteers being active and retired business executives and entrepreneurs.

Sole Proprietorship – A business that legally has no separate existence from its owner. Income and losses are taxed on the individual's personal income tax return. The sole proprietorship is the simplest business form under which one can operate a business. The sole proprietorship is not a legal entity.

Tax Haven – Generic term for geographical area outside the jurisdiction of one's home country which imposes only a few restriction on legitimate business activities within its jurisdiction, and little or no income tax. Also called a low tax jurisdiction, non tax jurisdiction, or offshore haven.

Business Terms & Definitions

Value Added Tax – A value added tax (VAT) is a consumption tax added to a product's sales price. It represents a tax on the "value added" to the product throughout its production process.

Wall Street – Wall Street is a street in lower Manhattan that is the original home of the New York Stock Exchange and the historic headquarters of the largest U.S. Brokerages and investment banks.

Yield – The yield is the income return on an investment, such as the interest or dividends received from holding a particular security. The yield is usually expressed as an annual percentage rate based on the investment's cost, current market value or face value.

Zero Interest Rates – A zero interest rate policy is a route taken by a central bank to keep the base rate at zero percent in an attempt to stimulate demand in the economy by making the supply of money cheaper.

$10,000 MegaSized Internet Marketing & Copy Writing & SEO Course & $1,000 Value Bonus

LIBRARY I (Video Training Programs)
1. Product Creation
2. Copy Writing & Payment
3. Auto Responder & Product Download Page
4. How to start a Freelancing business
5. Video Marketing
6. List Building
7. Affiliate Marketing
8. How to Get Massive Web Site Traffic

LIBRARY II (Video Training Programs)
1. Goldmine Government Grants
2. How to Write a Business Plan
3. Secrets to making money on eBay
4. Credit Repair
5. Goal Setting
6. Asset Protection How to Incorporate

$10,000 MegaSized Internet Marketing & Copy Writing & SEO Course & $1,000 Value Bonus

Library III
1. SEO SIMPLIFIED PART 1
2. SEO SIMPLIFIED PART 2
3. SEO Private Network Blogs
4. SEO Social Signals
5. SEO Profits

Bonus 1000 Package!
1. Insider Secrets to Government Contracts (PDF)
2. 1000 Books/Guides (text files)
3. Vacation Discounts (text file w/links to discounts)
4. Media Players (3 Software Programs)
100% MONEY BACK GUARANTEE!!!
ALL ON A 8 GIGABYTE FLASH DRIVE

This Massive Library with a $10,000 value all for only a
1 time payment of $67!!!
Get Instant Access by Using the Link Below:

https://urlzs.com/p7v3T

Leave a review and join Our VIP Mailing List Then Get All our Audio Books Free! We will be releasing over 100 money making audio books within the next 12 months! Just leave a review and join our mailing list and get them all for free!

Just Hit/Type in the Link Below

https://urlzs.com/HfbGF

www.ingramcontent.com/pod-product-compliance
Lightning Source LLC
Chambersburg PA
CBHW052113110526
44592CB00013B/1593